BOOK OF FOOTBALL STUFF

Other Books in This Series

BOOK OF BASEBALL STUFF

BOOK OF
Football
Stuff

Ron Martirano

Illustrated by Mike McCoy

imagine!
New York
www.imaginebks.com

Text and art copyright © 2010 by Imagine Publishing, Inc.

Published by Imagine Publishing, Inc.
25 Whitman Road, Morganville, NJ 07751

Distributed in the United States of America by
BookMasters Distribution Services, Inc.
30 Amberwood Parkway, Ashland, OH 44805

Distributed in Canada by
BookMasters Distribution Services, Inc.
c/o Jacqueline Gross Associates, 165 Dufferin Street,
Toronto, Ontario, Canada M6K 3H6

Distributed in the United Kingdom by
Publishers Group UK
8 The Arena, Mollison Avenue, Enfield, EN3 7NL, UK

ISBN-10: 0-9823064-0-7
ISBN-13: 978-0-9823064-0-6

Library of Congress Control Number: 2009922032

Designed by Marc Cheshire
Printed in China
1 3 5 7 9 10 8 6 4 2

To my stepfather Ron, my uncle Frank,
and every Sunday dinner cooked by my grandmother
that was interrupted by the Giants game

Contents

Introduction

Like the moment after a running back commits himself to a potential hole in the defensive line, football brings together opposing forces to create unforeseeable results. It is a strategic game orchestrated with tough guys in helmets by tougher guys holding clipboards, and it is as cerebral as it is physical. Week after week, tactics and violence come together to produce the incredible, and every now and then, they hit hard enough to force out a laugh as well. There should be nothing funny about a quarterback whose leg is broken on an endless slow-motion loop replayed for the country to squirm through over and over—until years later when the linebacker who broke it suggests that he should be thanked by the QB for all the mileage he got out of the story.

Like all sports, it is the stories left behind that give context to the stats in the record books. So many of the game's stories exist only as punch lines (the quarterback who gave himself a concussion celebrating a touchdown, the wide receiver who shot himself in the leg), that part of the fun in writing this book was connecting those one-liners back to the games. Yes, Eagles fans once booed Santa Claus, and yes, a defensive end once recovered a fumble and ran the wrong way. Sadly, not all game-time interactions and off-the-field hijinks are verifiable. Somewhere out there are stories I couldn't nail down, like the pass off the fingertips of its intended receiver or a Green Bay kicker who dared defy Vince Lombardi by faking a field goal to set up a touchdown and was then afraid to come off the field and face the iconic coach. Fortunately, so much of the game's history has been detailed and catalogued that many of the

Get over here. I'll show you how to kick!!!

myths, legends, and tall tales I grew up with (as well as those I saw unfold as a fan) could be matched to the plays that made them possible. Hopefully, the result returns a small, fun history of the game back to the Sunday afternoons (or Monday nights) when they were first experienced.

While the truth behind my mystery kicker unfortunately remained out of reach (if the story actually happened, it was most likely Don Chandler), the stories in the pages that follow not only capture the elements of the game but also lift those elements beyond the Xs, Os, and yellow Telestrator lines on your television set. You'll find no discourse of strategy or postgame analysis: Only moments that have lived on, including some of those whose principles would just assume they were forgotten. Victory and defeat are a given, but politics, history, business, oddballs, thugs, and stupidity all find

Eat the turkey or watch the turkeys.

their way inside the huddle—not to mention an end-less supply of football puns. So, in the tradition of fall and winter Sunday family gatherings in which meal-time conversations were punctuated (and occasionally hijacked) by the play-by-play calls of a nearby television set "accidentally" left on, I invite you to take a seat and thumb through an album of seasons past.

All the President's Linemen

"It's the sport of kings, better than diamond rings . . . football." —LL Cool J

LADIES may love "Cool" James, and while he might just have easily rapped about football as the sport of presidents, the unfortunate follow-up rhyme would have been much less flashy ("played by each state's residents?").

That said, many of those who have taken America's highest office have embraced the sport and its place in our culture above and beyond the nuclear football carried by their nearest military aide. Commissioner Pete Rozelle's decision to resume the football schedule within a week of the assassination of President John F. Kennedy (whose games of touch football on the White House lawn were a regular feature in Camelot) is for some, the gridiron equivalent of FDR's letter requesting that baseball be played during World War II—elevating the sport to a form of national escape and signifier of normalcy during difficult times.

While no one expects the President to throw out the "first pass" of the season, as football has taken its place atop the American sports culture, it comes as no surprise that many of the "men of the people" are fans of the game.

GETTING INVOLVED

Sure there are international crises and domestic dilemmas facing the president every day, but sometimes it's not enough for a him to play tag football on the lawn or watch the game from the stands. There are times when presidential leadership is required to keep players, coaches, and fans from really hurting themselves or institutions from really hurting the game we all love.

Throw Softly and Carry the Ball
for Big Yardage

The 1893 Army-Navy game was an all-out war in the stands. Navy won by a final score of 6-4, but the contest (which was also the first time a helmet, then made of leather, was worn on the field) incited numerous fights and an alleged incident that saw a rear admiral nearly duel a brigadier general. In attendance was President Grover Cleveland, who was so disturbed by the breakdown in behavior among military personnel that he called a cabinet meeting the following February. The results of which saw the Secretaries of the Navy and of War return to their respective institutions and inform the student body that there would be no more games between the two military academies.

The cease-fire lasted five years, until Teddy Roosevelt, then the Assistant Secretary of the Navy, got involved.

19

Well Bob, I think Army has a distinct advantage—it can attack from the ground and the air.

Roosevelt wrote a letter to the Secretary of War seeking to reinstitute the game (foreshadowing the WWII correspondence written over forty years later by his cousin FDR to the commissioner of baseball). In the letter, Roosevelt suggested academic standards for both teams be created to ensure that the contest be played for the further enrichment of the cadets on the field. It took another two years, but in 1899 the game resumed, and it has been played annually (and without interruption) for more than 100 years.

The Bully Pulpit in Action

Outdoorsman that he was, Teddy Roosevelt wasn't quite finished playing out his role in shaping football history. Three years into his presidency, it was quite clear that the college game needed a rough rider to knock it into shape. Stats for the 1905 season included almost 150

Football's too dangerous? I don't get it.

serious injuries and twenty-three deaths. As legend has it, T.R. was prompted to action by the photo of a bloody and beaten Robert "Tiny" Maxwell of Swarthmore in a Washington paper the day after a game against Penn. (By the way, Tiny wasn't tiny . . . wonder what the other team looked like.) Roosevelt threatened the leaders of college football that he'd have the sport abolished if they didn't reform. A meeting of the National Intercollegiate Football Conference (the precursor to the NCAA) followed, and the results reshaped the game.

Among the reforms inspired by Roosevelt's threats were unnecessary roughness rules that would see any player who slugged or beat on an opponent who was down, ejected with no substitute allowed to take his place for the rest of the half. Other changes included the creation of the neutral zone, reducing the game time from seventy to sixty minutes, and requiring teams to move the ball ten yards instead of five for a first down. Most significant was a new rule allowing for the completion of forward passes behind the line of scrimmage. Almost a decade would go by before the pass was used as an effective weapon, in an irony that must have delighted a Navy man like T.R., as quarterback Gus Dorais repeatedly connected with Knute Rockne of Notre Dame to upset Army in 1913.

A Voice for Change

Almost a century later, the fate of college football nation can only hope that President Barack Obama, whose administration has already seen countless comparisons to FDR with the economic crisis and recession they have had to face, can invoke Teddy as well. On the eve of the election, Obama was interviewed on ESPN and asked what he would change about modern sports. In line with the majority that would elect him to office, the Illinois senator called for a playoff system to replace the controversial BCS in determining the national college champion. (In the interest of fair time, Senator John McCain, given the same forum, discussed performance-enhancing drugs). The BCS was as receptive to Obama's suggestion as an opposition party, but in a campaign won on "hope," change is hopefully something we can all still believe in.

"I AM NOT A COACH"

Questioning Richard Nixon's judgment was a multi-generational pastime. From the questions that swirled around his campaign finances in the '50s to his role in the Watergate break-ins and the subsequent cover-up, having Dick Nixon to kick around was as American as apple pie. From the counterculture's resistance to the silent majority's approval, neither could deny that a president who once reserved a phone line to receive the play-by-play of a Cowboy-Redskin game was, if nothing else, a diehard football fan.

The President's Playbook

During the 1971 season, Nixon reached out to Redskins head coach George Allen, an acquaintance from Nixon's days as a congressman, and offered encouragement and support after a season-opening loss. When the Skins slipped into an 0-2 hole, Allen asked the President if he would make a practice appearance to lift team spirits. Nixon obliged, commuting via helicopter to the team's practice field at Redskin Park and impressing the players with his knowledge of stats and formations. In gratitude, Allen turned the Skins over to the Nixon and allowed him to call a play during practice—a reverse.

One moment Prime Minister, it's 3rd and goal.

The play was successful, as was the team in the weeks that followed, winning that weekend and making their way to their first playoff berth in twenty-five years as they faced the 49ers the day after Christmas.

Up 10-3 and poised to score once more in the closing minutes of the first half, Allen called a reverse to his wide receiver that resulted in a loss of yardage. The team missed the subsequent field goal, lost the game 24-20, and the game's crucial moment was immediately linked to Nixon's practice play earlier in the season.

Dubbed "Nixon's Play," the story took on a life of its own, with tall tales of Nixon regularly phoning in plays to Allen and the Commander in Chief putting his stamp on the Skins the following year during Super Bowl VII. Columnist Art Buchwald teased, "If George Allen doesn't accept any more plays from Richard Nixon, he may go down in history as one of pro football's greatest coaches." Neither coach nor president confirmed nor denied the stories. Years later, Allen's daughter Jennifer penned a column for ESPN's Page 2, pointing out that her father simply wasn't the type to take advice from outsiders, be they presidents or anyone else.

The Package Is Thirsty

While Nixon clearly enjoyed a close friendship with Allen, his impact on the game was limited to practices only, though controversy could clearly not care less whether there was an official game on the schedule. Years before the infamous reverse call, while Allen was coaching in Los Angeles, then-candidate Nixon took a stop along the campaign trail in California to attend a Rams preseason game against the Chiefs. The coach sent his son Bruce into the stands to keep his political friend company, delivering roster cards and sodas with his compliments. During the game, Bruce recognized the Chiefs' offensive formation and jumped up, yelling, "Shotgun!" Needless to say the Secret Service was not amused.

MOST VIGOROUS PRESIDENT

For many, Gerald Ford's legacy as the 38th President of the United States is either hitched to his pardon of Nixon or Chevy Chase's immortal spoofs of his clumsiness on *Saturday Night Live*. While it's true that Ford may have had his issues with overhead doors and airplane steps, he was still, without question, the most athletically accomplished president.

I Could Have Been Someone

While his successor, Ronald Reagan, played the part of the Gipper in the biography of Notre Dame's Knute Rockne, it was Ford who had the All-American life as a football player. A scholarship player at the University of Michigan, the future president took part in two undefeated seasons with the Wolverines as a linebacker and center, culminating in a pair of national championships. During that time, he earned the distinction of becoming the only future American president to tackle a Heisman trophy winner (the very first Heisman recipient at that), after bringing down Jay Berwanger, captain of the University of Chicago Maroons. Ford was honored as the team's MVP in 1934 and played in the '35 college all-star game (now known as the East-West Shrine Game). Ford even had a chance to go pro, with both the Lions and the Packers in need of a good lineman, but he rejected their contract offers in favor of law school at Yale. By his own account, "If I had gone into professional football, the name Jerry Ford might have been a household name today."

Executive Huddle

After his presidency, Ford would visit his alma mater from time to time. He stopped going to games once he

*Referees called the play back—too many
Secret Service men on the field.*

realized that with all the well-wishers looking to shake his hand, he rarely got to do what he wanted—watch the game. He did get some executive privileges to make up for it. With permission from legendary UM head coach Bo Schembechler, Ford would visit during team practices and lean into the huddle. With a Secret Service agent hanging over the former President's shoulder, a concerned UM quarterback once asked Schembechler what to do if the agent got in the way of the ball. Schembechler's response: "Run over him."

THE PLAYOFF CHOKE

Unbeknownst to the defending Super Bowl champion Ravens when they came to Miami in 2002 for the AFC Wild Card game, the fate of the nation hung in the balance of their playoff contest.

The Lone Snack Food

While Baltimore was on their way to routing the Dolphins 20-3, a most twisted fiend was positioned to add its name to a short list of historical footnotes whose most notable members include Richard Lawrence; John Hinckley, Jr.; and Squeaky Fromme. With the likes of Abraham Zapruder nowhere to be found, thus no film to chronicle the specifics, the evening's timeline is fuzzy at best. What is known is that although the identity of the would-be assassin was never confirmed, persons of interest include the likes of Bachman, Snyder (of Hanover), and a mysterious shadow figure going by the alias of "Aunt Annie." By the time the final whistle had blown, one of these alleged conspirators would see themselves added to the ranks of those who had attempted to kill the President of the United States and failed, when, with neither Secret Service nor Heimlich practitioner to intercede, the leader of the free world choked on a pretzel.

President George W. Bush was in the comfort of the White House bedroom when the events unfolded.

Perhaps it was his own gag reflex at the sight of Miami's nonexistent defense and futile running game that made him vulnerable to attack. The pretzel in question was one of many being consumed during the game; only this one "did not go down right," causing the president to lose consciousness and fall off his couch. Bush came to on the floor moments later, the recipient of a pair of bruises on his face and some funny looks from his dogs. Afterwards, the 42nd President suggested that had he only listened to his mother's advice to, "chew your pretzels before you swallow," the near crisis could have been avoided.

MY FELLOW AMERICANS

Then-senatorial candidate Barack Obama emerged onto the national scene in 2004, when his keynote speech before the Democratic National Committee launched him to political stardom. Two years later, the hype around the Illinois senator had taken on a life of its own, and his name was regularly being invoked among possible 2008 presidential candidates.

Monday Night Campaigning

In December of 2006, with speculation running rampant, Obama decided it was time to address the nation, releasing a statement that before that evening's *Monday Night Football* game, he would be making an announcement, "about an upcoming contest of great importance to the American people." As the Bears took the field against the Rams, and with the country watching, the future President spoke directly to the American people.

"Tonight I'd like to put all the doubts to rest," Obama began. "After a lot of thought and a good deal of soul-searching, I would like to announce to my hometown of

Chicago and all of America that I'm ready." After a beat, he continued, "For the Bears to go all the way!" History would show that Obama's next major announcement, the declaration of his candidacy for president the following May, would be the wiser venture, as the Bears fell just short of serving the first fan when they lost to Indianapolis in Super Bowl XLI.

The Stuff of Champions

EVERY play in the book, every hit on Saturday and Sunday, every inch fought for off the line of scrimmage . . . each is played toward one goal. Herm Edwards summed it up when he said, "You play to win the game," and if you win enough, you get your shot at a championship ring.

At one point, Dan Marino seemed to possess every record a quarterback could, but years after his retirement, it's rare that his name gets mentioned without reference to the fact that he never won it all. Meanwhile Eli Manning went from Peyton's overrated little brother to Super Bowl MVP overnight. Once it's proven that you can win when it counts, everything that precedes it is rewritten as steps along the journey.

One way to look at it is this: The true champions win the last game of the season. Everyone else goes home and waits for next year.

PRE GAME

Big games run on hype and preparation. The week leading up to a playoff or championship contest is charged with media stories playing up perceived strengths and weaknesses and stirring up controversy whenever possible. Bulletin-board quotes fire up the opposition, and with each passing day, the narrative expands, providing the sixty minutes of on-the-field action with a seven-day prelude that shapes the story and how we remember the game.

Mayoral Name Change

Although rarely discussed in official conversations, gambling is certainly an integral part of football's culture, and outside of the commonplace world of underdogs and point spreads, there is no more accepted wager in all of sport than the mayoral bet. City A and City B face off in a key game, City A's mayor bets some local product against something of equal value from City B to prove to the constituency his or her unwavering faith in the team's ability to throttle their rivals. The problem with "unwavering faith" is that it's hard to have it taken seriously as a fan when you share a name with the opposing team. Just as Mr. Packer gets no love in Chicago, Mayor Luke Ravenstahl of Pittsburgh had something of a crisis at hand when the Steelers faced the Baltimore Ravens in the 2009 AFC Championship Game.

Ravenstahl is a lifelong Steelers fan, with a stadium fight that required police intervention in 2005 among his diehard credentials. Added to the top of that list is his trip to the Alleghany County Department of Court Records, where he filled out the paperwork to have his name legally changed to "Steelerstahl" before the Steelers-Ravens game. Fanatical? Perhaps. But the press alone beats any amount of Maryland crab cakes one elected official could carry. The Steelers won the game 23-4, taking home the Lamar Hunt Trophy for the seventh time en route to facing the Cardinals in Super Bowl XLIII. The next day, Mayor Steelerstahl became Ravenstahl once again, having never paid the application fee. Hmm . . . election year? You bet.

The Original Spygate

In the early nineties, over a decade before Bill Belichick's fondness for secret video of the opposition became public knowledge, Jimmy Johnson had some special footage of his own to help him take on the Bills in the Super Bowl.

The Cowboys played and beat Buffalo in the championship game two years in a row, outscoring the Bills 82-30, so it's fair to say that neither Johnson nor his team needed that much help. As Johnson tells the story, in the week leading up to one of the Super Bowl games, a television crew had gone down to cover the Bills while they practiced. That night, Johnson was watching when the piece on the Bills came on the air. The Dallas head coach paid immediate attention when he noticed a formation he had never seen, used in a throwaway, B-roll shot. Absent from the hours of game tape the Cowboys had studied, Buffalo head coach, Marv Levy, had been working on something new, only to have the cameras pick it up and broadcast it.

When the two teams met a few days later, Johnson and the Cowboys were ready, and while neither game hinged on a single play, scouting the opposition off the evening news and being able to spoil Levy's attempt to catch Dallas off guard, was the perfect feather in Johnson's perfectly coifed cap.

One player who could have used some advanced video to help Dallas run their combined score up even further was Cowboy defensive lineman Leon Lett. If Buffalo had practiced their post-fumble response to showboating players about to score their first touchdown since Pee Wee football, it might have spared Lott some embarrassment.

During the fourth quarter of Super Bowl XX-VII (the first between the two teams), Lett recovered a Frank Reich fumble and had a wide-open field all to himself. While approaching the end zone, Lett began celebrating a little too early, never seeing Bills wide receiver Don Beebe who came from behind and knocked the ball out of Lett's hands, resulting in a touchback. After the game, when Dallas was being presented with the Lombardi trophy, Lott received the prize with two hands and declared, "I won't drop this one."

GLORY BOUND

The Promised Land isn't found easily, but the road to it has as much to do with defining a champion as does the ring and the trophy on the other side of the final score. Big wins aren't big without a season's worth of challenges to hoist them up, and at the same time, each step along the way has the potential to be remembered as a turning point toward something great.

Miracle at the Meadowlands

In 1978, the Giants and the Eagles were at something of a crossroads. The storied New York franchise was a shadow of the team that once dominated the pre-NFL merger landscape. The Eagles were vying for their first playoff appearance in eighteen years, as Philadelphia had not been to the big game since winning the 1960 NFL Championship. When the two teams met in

November, Philly was 7-5 and in contention for a wild card berth. Up 17-12 with less than two minutes to go in the game, the Giants recovered a fumble against their rivals, who had no time-outs left, all but ensuring a New York victory and another failed season for Philadelphia.

All the Giants had to do was run out the clock, but it had been a physical game between the two teams, and instead, New York chose to run on the Eagles' defensive line for a little payback. With thirty-one seconds left, in what should have been the game's last play, New York set for one more run, only to fumble the snap. Herm Edwards, who would someday call the Meadowlands home as head coach of the New York Jets, was then a safety for the Eagles. Blitzing on the snap, Edwards described himself as being in the right place at the right time and had the loose ball in his sight. According to Edwards, "Generally they teach you in football that

Oh well, lost another one.

when the ball is on the ground you're supposed to fall on the ball. Well, if I would have fallen on the ball at that point, the game would have ended. So I just decided to pick it up and run with it." A stunned and silenced New York crowd watched in horror as he did just that, recovering the fumble and running the ball in for a touchdown, giving the Eagles a 19-17 victory. The win lifted Philadelphia emotionally, and according to Edwards, the "miracle" play helped the team regain a lot of confidence. It also proved to be the difference in their playoff pursuit, as Philly took the Wild Card by a single game.

As for the Giants, it was a low point in the team's history, but in their embarrassment, the play proved to be the catalyst in turning the team around and building the championship team of the eighties. Another unintended effect was felt at every level of the game, as from that point forward, the standard formation for game-ending plays, such as a quarterback taking a knee to run out the clock, would include positioning a tackle behind the QB . . . just in case.

Head North Young Man

Doug Flutie was too short to be a NFL quarterback, or so he'd been told. Players of his size couldn't see over the pocket, they couldn't find players down field. . . . Quite simply, they were far from the ideal. All this was of no comfort to the University of Miami after the 1984 Orange Bowl. With twenty-eight seconds on the clock, Flutie's Boston College Eagles got the ball back at their own 20-yard line, down 45-41. It took the 5-foot, 9-inch quarterback twenty-two seconds just to get the ball to midfield, leaving him one play to answer prayers across Boston and complete an improbable comeback.

He was a man among giants. A tiny man.

The prayers were answered, as Flutie's forty-eight-yard, Hail Mary pass gave the Eagles a 47-45 victory.

Despite running away with the Heisman trophy, after graduation, Flutie bounced around the USFL and the

NFL for a pair of seasons without getting enough of a shot to take off as a starter. He finally signed on with the Calgary Stampeders of the CFL. When he met the team's offensive coordinator John Hufnagel, he was able to demonstrate the type of competitor he was for his new team before running a single play. The two got together for a one-on-one basketball game, and Hufnagel jumped out to a 13-2 lead. Flutie won the game 15-13. He went on to win for the Stampeders as well, leading the team to three Grey Cup Championships, each time as the MVP. He also took home the league's most outstanding player honors a record six times. He came back to the NFL in 1998, and earned Pro Bowl honors as well as the league's Comeback Player of the Year Award.

THE BIG GAME

After the buildup and the chatter, the predictions and

the bets, and once the clock starts, it's the same game it always is. The stakes don't change the size of the ball or the dimensions of the field, but they do erect a giant magnifying glass under which all the action unfolds, to be reviewed, dissected, and relived in the years to follow. Field goals are made and missed every week, yet Adam Vinatieri is a legend in New England while Scott Norwood lives in infamy in Buffalo. Whether it's a clutch split of the uprights or wide right, it will be remembered.

Too Many Men on the Field

The 1958 Championship game between the New York Giants and the Baltimore Colts is widely considered to be "the greatest game ever played." What set it apart beyond the action on the field was the effect it had on the sport. For the first time, interest in professional football's title, and the game itself, reached a level that put it alongside baseball as an event worthy of the nation's attention. It had taken the league years to escape the shadow of the college game, credited in part to the rule change that allowed unlimited substitutions in the NFL while their NCAA counterparts prohibited the same. And with the excitement generated over the '58 crown, the pros were now poised to take their place as the premier sport in the country.

The game featured seventeen future hall of famers, among them thirteen players, three coaches (Vince Lombardi and Tom Landry as assistants for the Giants, and Weeb Ewbank, the Colts' head coach), and the owner and future owner of the Giants, Tim and Wellington Mara. On the field, a 14-3 Colts advantage at halftime was quickly erased by the start of the fourth quarter, as the Giants pulled ahead 17-14 on a Frank Gifford touchdown reception. When Baltimore tied it up with a few seconds left on the clock, it marked the debut of sudden-death overtime football in the NFL. Shades of Eagles quarterback Donovan McNabb's publicized ignorance of the rules forty years later, the players began counting a split of the winner's payout in their heads, unaware of the extra quarter that awaited them. After a three-and-out set by New York on their first possession, legendary Colts quarterback Johnny Unitas took the ball over at Baltimore's 20-yard line and began a historic drive that would keep the 60,000+ in attendance at Yankee Stadium, and the millions watching from home, riveted to the action. Unfortunately for the viewers in their living room, the excited fans pulled the plug on the action.

As Unitas and the Colts marched down the field, the crowd got swept up in the action and began climbing out of their seats, accidentally disconnecting NBC's power feed. For the rest of the country, Baltimore's drive was suddenly replaced with the snows of signal failure. Even worse, with no lines of communication between the booth and the refs, the officials had no idea what was going on. The game was about to continue when those in the stands saw what looked like one of their own running on the field. The man seemed to be drunk as he weaved his way across the turf, evading security and drawing laughs from the crowd and the ire of sportswriters covering the game. Not all of the media in attendance were offended. The NBC crew used the time to reestablish their connection, and sportscaster Lindsey Nelson recognized the "drunk" for who he was, Stan Rotkiewicz. As an NBC business manager, Rotkiewicz would have known better than anyone else that what was about to transpire could have potentially been

Oops. Bah, who needs TV anyway!

one of the biggest moments in the history of the game. To have millions of home viewers across the nation miss out on the outcome of a game that had not only been heavily hyped, but was actually going to deliver, would have been disastrous. So for three minutes, Rotkiewicz stalled the game, finally leaving the field after the game was back on the air. Two plays later, the country watched along as the Colts became national champions.

Ice, Ice, Baby

The Ice Bowl stands among the storied games of the NFL's past as a testament to the toughness of the league and its players. The grueling conditions in which Dallas met Green Bay for the 1962 NFL Championship and a ticket to what would be remembered as Super Bowl II (the name "Super Bowl" would not be officially adopted for another year) have been well documented.

Temperatures of -13°F at kickoff and wind speeds at thirty miles per hour produced a -48°F wind-chill factor for the contest. A recently installed electric ground heating system was too weak to combat the Arctic blast and needed to be shut down as the excessive runoff risked explosive results. In killing the power, standing water was left on the field, which produced condensation against the tarps that promptly froze over, creating the gridiron equivalent of an ice-skating rink for the game to be played upon. In addition, the referees' whistles froze, as did the focus wheels on the television cameras, along with cups of coffee in the press box—never mind the sellout crowd of frenzied (if not frigid) fans. The weather didn't stop the home team, as Green Bay pulled out a brilliant last-minute drive to take the game and the league title, and put themselves on the road to their third straight championship.

*The linebacker's triple toe loop at the 20-yard line cost them
the game, even as the judges awarded him a 5.8.*

Author Jeff Davis uncovered an incredible footnote to
the game, as members of CBS's crew chartered a flight
to Chicago. Among them was future hall of famer Frank
Gifford and future baseball hall of fame and radio hall

of fame broadcaster Jack Buck. Gifford was seated next to the pilot at takeoff, and at an altitude of about 500 feet, the door next to him flew open. It wasn't secured and neither was Gifford. Having neglected to put on his safety belt, he found himself being pulled toward the open door and the open sky outside. Tom Brookshire, a former defensive back and fine broadcaster in his own right, was also onboard the four-seat Piper. Brookshire grabbed Gifford by the neck of his jacket to keep him from falling to a certain death. Gifford, struggling both to stay onboard and shut the door behind him, pulled the door so hard that he broke a strut on the plane.

Fortunately for all, the pilot was an experienced crop duster and was able to bring the plane down on a nearby strip in spite of the broken strut, the controls that were now starting to freeze up, and the halfback-turned-commentator hanging out of his door. Safe on the ground, the group was later able to enjoy a laugh at Buck's expense, who, during the height of the drama, without realizing the severity of the situation, yelled out to Brookshire, "Let him go! We'll do the commercial he's doing."

Front Office Tensions

The NFL has hosted its share of rivalries over the years, from Chicago and Green Bay to New York and Dallas, but Rozelle and Davis has a historic perch among the league's annals. There was bad blood between the two going back to the merger between the NFL, led by Rozelle, and the AFL, led by Davis. Davis blamed Rozelle for the terms of the merger in so much that his position of authority was erased as a result of it. Legal battles would later pit Davis' Raiders against the league when he tried to move the team out of Oakland.

The battles between the two, legal and otherwise, came to a head in 1980 when Rozelle seemingly shut down Davis' exit strategy from Oakland after a 22-0 league vote against relocating the team. (The wily owner eventually found a way to defy the commissioner's wishes and made his move two years later.) On the heels of the unanimous vote, the Raiders turned the corner as a team and found themselves playoff bound. Oakland squeezed passed Cleveland in the playoffs, and then knocked off their division rivals in San Diego (an especially satisfying win for Davis, as San Diego was a vocal opponent of any team playing out of Los Angeles who might poach their market), earning them the AFC crown and a ticket to the Super Bowl. Immediately, the press began to wonder what might happen if the Raiders won. It was the commissioner's right, and honor, to present the title trophy to the winning team's owner,

Catch this!

and any such interaction between Davis and Rozelle was bound to be awkward. The speculation proved prophetic, as Oakland defeated the Eagles 27-10. In the locker room after the game, a gracious Rozelle served up the Lombardi to a respectful Davis. Of course, Rozelle held the hardware with two hands before handing it over, thus avoiding a handshake. Years later, when Rozelle shocked a room full of gathered owners by announcing his retirement, it was Davis who went out of his way to catch Rozelle and offer up his hand before his old rival could leave.

The Cup Runneth Over

While the Canadian Football League didn't come to be until the 1950s, the Grey Cup, its championship prize, is over a century old and stands as Canada's oldest professional sports trophy. Like a veteran player, the title

*$50,000 or you'll never see the cup again . . . $25,000? $10,000?
Okay, I'll pay you $500, but you'll have to come get it.*

piece has taken its share of hits over the years, enduring far more than Lord Albert Henry Earl Grey ever envisioned when he had it commissioned in 1909. A rundown of award adventures includes a kidnapping in 1969 when, after being stolen from Landsowne Park in Ottawa, a ransom was called in.

The league refused to pay, and the cup was eventually found unharmed. Twenty years prior it had also survived a fire that broke out while it was on display at the Toronto Argonauts Rowing Club. Its luck would begin to fade in the 1990s when Edmonton's Blake Dermott head butted it, leaving a mark on both the trophy and Dermott's head. When the Montreal Alouettes won it all in 2002, they partied a little too hard with the coveted hardware and returned it in pieces. Reassembled, the British Columbia Lions didn't even have the chance to party hard, as Kelly Bates snapped the trophy in two while shaking it in victory after BC won it all in 2006.

Catch-42

Boston was in the middle of a very good year. The Red Sox had won their second World Series title in four years. The Celtics were the hottest team in the NBA after a flurry of offseason moves (and would eventually capture their league title). And in the middle of it all, as the heavy jewel of the would-be triple crown, was the New England Patriots, knocking on history's door. Only the 1972 Dolphins had won the Super Bowl after going undefeated through the regular season—a perfect 17-0. Over thirty-five years later, with an expanded schedule, the heavily favored Patriots sat at 18-0 and only needed to get by the underdog Giants to complete what could have been one of the greatest trifectas in sports history.

Down 10-7 in the fourth quarter, New England

New England didn't cheer when this circus came to town.

pulled ahead on a Brady-to-Moss connection, standing less than three minutes away from immortality. The Boston Globe already had a book listed on Amazon.com titled 19-0, and it's safe to say that '72 Dolphins' running back Mercury Morris, who once said not to talk to him about another team going undefeated until they were "on my block," could hear the moving vans. The Giants got the ball back, and on a third and five from their own 44-yard line, rewrote history. Quarterback Eli Manning was looking for David Tyree on a post pattern when the pocket around him started to collapse. Manning scrambled, somehow evading Patriots linebacker Adalius Thomas who was clutching his jersey. The Giants quarterback broke free, rolled out, and let the ball fly. Four years out of Syracuse University, David Tyree had only four receptions for thirty-five combined yards during the 2007 regular season. When Manning's fourth quarter pass came his way, Tyree leaped and pinned the ball to the top of his helmet, completing one of the most incredible catches in Super Bowl history, preserving the Giants final drive, and topping off a solid day for the receiver who had caught the only New York touchdown to that point. Three plays later, there was no chance New York would shoot themselves in the foot and waste the Tyree-inspired momentum, as Plaxico Burress caught the go-ahead touchdown to put the Giants ahead for good, 17-14.

Manning to Tyree was a "circus catch," a "miracle," and more. It was a helmet catch to knock loose the prized jewel from Boston's triple crown. In the end, it was also, most likely, all that stood between 19-0 and 18-1.

Smashmouth Stuff

**HETHER** it's the violent action that defines much of the game, the pedestal upon which its stars are placed, or the mentality that allows all involved to gear themselves up for weekly contests, football produces its own breed. In baseball, every play hinges on what happens after a ball is thrown at a batter. Millions of variations involving hit batters, hit animals, and anything else related to flying projectiles are part of the fabric of the game. In football, every play begins with a collision of human bodies at the line of scrimmage. The results not only influence the kinds of characters who emerge, but also the specific flavor of random events unique to the gridiron.

TOUGH BREAKS

Hard, bone-crushing hits are as much a part of football

as tight spirals and Gatorade showers. For there to be an "unnecessary roughness" penalty call, there must first be a level of necessary roughness that permeates each and every set of downs. With so much roughing, it comes as no surprise when even the safest moments of the game are an occasion for injury.

Tails You Lose

Turk Edwards was a tackle during the thirties with a reputation for durability. During his era, a 6-foot, 2-inch, 255-pound tackle stood out for his size, and Edwards made the most of what he had. Adjectives such as "steamrolling," "immovable," "impregnable," and "smothering" were all applied to the workhorse player and one time Pro Bowler, whose nickname was the "Rock of Gibraltar." He was also one of the fastest players in the league at the time, adding considerable force to his hard hits. An eventual hall of famer, he came up with the Boston Braves and moved with the team to finish his career in Washington. The "finish" was something of a freak occurrence during the second game of the 1940 season against the New York Giants. Weeks prior to the season's start, Edwards was asked about his conditioning and preparedness for the upcoming schedule of games. "I feel as good as ever," he said.

Edwards began the game with New York by meeting future hall of fame center Mel Hein at midfield. The two shook hands, Edwards whirled around to turn back toward the Redskins' bench, and in one motion the seemingly indestructible "bouncing boulder" twisted his knee, effectively ending his career on a coin toss.

Playing With Your Head

Gus Frerotte was first in the league with more yards

per completed pass than any other quarterback in 1995 (13.8). He was sent to the Pro Bowl in 1996. In 2008, he was a part of the longest completed pass of the season at 99 yards. Frerotte played as a starting quarterback in Washington, Detroit, Cincinnati, Minnesota, Miami, and St. Louis.

While his resume won't get him a ticket to Canton and an invite to the Hall of Fame as anything but a guest, Gus Frerotte still lived out the dream of millions of high school players and armchair spectators. That aside, he will always be remembered for being the QB who knocked himself out of a game.

In November 1997, the Redskins met the Giants for the first round of their annual home and away NFC East battle. During the second quarter of a scoreless game, Frerotte rolled out on a third and goal from the 1-yard line, only to dash for the end zone and score what would be Washington's only points of the afternoon. Frerotte was clearly pleased with himself, running to the corner of the stadium, celebrating with the Washington faithful, and spiking the ball.

Then things got weird.

Swept up in the moment, Frerotte banged his head against the wall. With his helmet on, against a padded wall, he still created enough of an impact for his body to recoil after the self-inflicted hit. His coaches and staff saw him wince while removing his helmet, and after briefly returning to the game, he wound up below the stadium getting X-rayed before being shipped off to the local hospital for further study. Jeff Hostettler, who had won Super Bowl XXV for New York, finished the game for Washington, a 7-7 tie. Meanwhile, Frerotte had a sprained neck, a bruised ego, and a story he would never live down.

Happy Anniversary . . . Um . . . What's Your Name?

Wide receiver Ed McCaffrey is known for his three Super Bowl rings, one Pro Bowl appearance, and being one of John Elway's favorite targets for the Denver Broncos. He's also known for not fumbling a ball after an amazing catch, even though his leg was being broken in a few different places while he was making it.

Now, injuries are not only worrisome for those on the field and in the stands, but also for those watching at home, including the player's family. But, perhaps like the boy who cried wolf, after a while, you learn to live with it, often with humor. In 1999 when McCaffrey (who was well known for taking a beating on the field) suffered yet another concussion, his nonchalant wife said, "When he didn't remember our anniversary, I knew he was okay."

TOUGH GUYS

With bodily harm potentially on the heels of every snap, it takes a true athletic warrior to step up to the line each time a play is called and be willing to cross it on command. The toughest players not only enjoy a physical advantage, but a psychological one as well. They are planned for and obsessed over, and their presence on the opposing roster is enough to keep anyone up at night.

The Fine Line Between Tough and Crazy

When asked about Tim Rossovich, the one-time Pro Bowl defensive end for the Eagles, Chargers, and Oilers, his friends will most often field questions that begin with, "Is it true?"

"Is it true that he once set himself ablaze, walked into a party, had the host and other guests put the flames out, and then stood up and announced he was at the wrong address and walked out without another word?"

"Is it true that he once lathered himself in shaving cream and went streaking across his college campus?"

"Is it true that he once hid a baby sparrow in his mouth and let it free mid-conversation?" Or that he walked around in a Dracula cape and wizard's outfit, that he regularly stood on his head while immersing it in a bucket of ice water, that he once did a backflip into a cake to liven up a party, or even that he took it upon himself to act as a freelance scare agent at a haunted house ride at Disneyland?

Repeatedly, the answer is, "Yes, it's true." Rossovich was one of the NFL's more unique characters. But his eccentricities didn't make him a total flake. When he wasn't diving into the Eagles' whirlpool (indifferent to whether or not it was occupied), Rossovich was a fighter and a team leader. He played with ferocious intensity,

Have any of you guys seen Rossovich?
He said he was going to drop by after the game.

driving tackle sleds into the ground and then punishing them for having the audacity to have stood in his way. He fought with the opposition (and teammates), apologizing to offensive linemen moments before he flattened them.

A true competitor, Rossovich once took on one of the NFL's toughest tough guys, Mike Ditka. The contest was to see who could open the most bottles with their teeth. Rossovich was ahead 100-3 when he started eating the glass. Ditka conceded the contest.

When He Was Just a Wee Pebble

Perhaps you know him as a multiple WWF (now the WWE) champion. Or, you've seen him in one of his several successful movies: *The Scorpion King, Get Smart, Race to Witch Mountain*, along with many others. But before Dwayne Johnson became "The Rock"—one of the most successful pro wrestlers ever—and then became Dwayne Johnson again (this time as an A-list movie star), Dwayne "The Rock" Johnson played football. In fact, in his senior year at his Bethlehem, Pennsylvania high school, he was a standout star who was named to *USA Today*'s All-American team and was considered one of the top ten high school defensive backs in the nation. Johnson chose to play for the Miami Hurricanes, and was part of the 1991 championship team his freshman year. And while he may be remembered for once trying to rip an opposing player's tongue out (he was tired of choking him), or maybe even for some inspiring defense, Johnson will probably be best remembered for running after an opposing team's mascot.

The incident started off as a bench-clearing fight between brawl-prone Miami and San Diego State. Not content to beat on the opposing players, Johnson saw San Diego's mascot, a man dressed up as a giant Aztec warrior (complete with sword), taunting the Miami players along Miami's own sideline. Johnson went after him, yelling, "I'll kill you! I'll kill you!" The Aztec must have had a good head start since he reached the safety of the stands before the defensive tackle could grab him. Years later, the more laid-back, role model recalled the incident: "Mom saw it . . . I embarrassed her; I embarrassed myself. What am I doing? I'm chasing a mascot! My helmet is off. . . . Thank goodness I didn't catch him." Oh yeah, it was a nationally televised game, and a clip of his burst of madness made the rounds of all the sports news outlets. At least he didn't grab for one of the sideline folding chairs.

By the way, a back injury limited Johnson's pro career to a short stint in the CFL (where he was teammates with Doug Flutie).

Where's my folding chair when I need it?

A Hard Day's Night

In the moments after the ball was snapped, Lawrence Taylor's level of play has been described as that of "a man among boys." During the eighties, as opponents prepared their pass protection schemes in the week leading up to a game, Taylor was the hurricane moving up the map that linemen and quarterbacks needed to board up the windows for, with no doubt as to whether or not he would hit, only how much damage would be left in his wake. Look no further than Redskin quarterback Joe Theismann, whose leg was broken and career ended by an LT sack on national television during a 1985 Monday night game.

LT was as much a force off the field as he was on the line, redefining the work-life balance with all-night benders that ran over into the early hours of game day that still left him fresh enough to put up what would have been career numbers for anyone else. Taylor was just as competitive in his postgame activities as he was on the gridiron. In his autobiography, he hinted at the strategic benefits of sending women to "hot" players on opposing teams the night before a game so they'd be worn out by the time they took the field—knowing that his competitors couldn't party as hard as he could and still be ready the next day. One time, after his brother came to visit and the two had a night out, LT was nowhere to be found come pregame. His teammates discovered him passed out in his hotel room. They propped him up, dressed him, and got him to drink coffee as they walked him down to the field. LT finished the day with four sacks.

The problem with such late-night activities was that the Giants had a curfew. Coaches would regularly inspect the players' hotel rooms for a nightly bed check, and Coach Bill Belichick, especially, had no problem handing out fines of up to $2,000 for those caught breaking the rules. By LT's own account, during training camp, it would be a miracle if he stayed in his room even one night a week. Getting away the other six required sneaking out. Surviving the inspections was easy enough. While some players left blow-up dolls in their beds so the coaches would think a real sleeping body was beneath the sheets, LT would pay the Giants' ball boy to lie in his bed and grunt when the coaches opened the door. Of course, with the bed covered, getting out of the building was still its own chore. One time, while making their way out the back door for a night on the town, LT and teammate Casey Merrill heard a noise. Thinking for a moment that they might be caught, they paused, only relaxing when they saw the source of the sound. It was future hall of famer, Harry Carson, sneaking back in.

Giving It All for the Game

Ronnie Lott was one of the toughest defensive backs to play the game, and anyone who doubted it just needed to shake his hand. From 1981 to 1994, Lott owned the secondary, first as a cornerback and eventually as a safety. Over the course of his career, he was all-pro eight times at three different positions (cornerback, free safety, and strong safety). Statistically, Lott racked up five 100-plus tackle seasons with over 1,000 career tackles, and twice led the league in interceptions and interceptions returned for touchdowns (beginning his rookie season with San Francisco where three of those TDs helped San Francisco get to the Super Bowl and almost won him the rookie of the year—Lott finished second to Lawrence Taylor). Lott started in twenty playoff games over the course of his career, with a shared record of nine postseason interceptions, en route to four

Put me in coach, I'm ready to play.

championship rings. It's safe to say Lott gave more than 100%. He gave 110% . . . and a pinky.

The 49ers closed out the 1985 season with a pair of games against the Cowboys and the Giants. During the

Dallas game, Lott was involved in a play that forever cemented his reputation as one of the toughest players in the game, and created a legend that took on a life of its own. While trying to take down Dallas fullback Timmy Newsome, the hall of fame cornerback's finger got caught on his chest, leaving his hand in an awkward position when his body collided with Newsome's helmet. By Lott's account, "My chest acted like an anvil upon impact," and the results weren't pretty. When the play was over, his pinky was mangled.

The story that emerged was that Lott went into the locker room and faced with having the pain of his broken digit impact his play, Lott made a seemingly impossible decision right on the spot. The truth is that Lott had his fingers wrapped in tape, and he played through the team's finale against the Giants before having the injury assessed during the offseason. The prognosis was that part of the bone was missing, left on the playing field, and the remaining pieces would never fuse back together. He was presented with two options. The first was an operation that would have required having a piece of bone removed from his wrist and grafted on to his finger, held in place with pins. It required possibly missing a few games the following season as well as being vulnerable to re-aggravating the injury. The second option: Cut off the tip of the broken pinky and play ball.

One season and nine-and-a-half fingers later, Lott earned his third of ten Pro Bowl invitations.

TOUGH CALLS

You're watching your favorite team on television, and they have just scored a touchdown on a particularly astounding play. (Who knew the Statue of Liberty play still worked!) The whole offense is jumping up and down when the camera quickly shifts to a little yellow piece of cloth on the field. You hold your breath as the officials confer. You're praying the call is against the defense. It's so quiet you can hear the announcers sweating. The official turns on his microphone and . . . not only is the touchdown called back, but the holding penalty sends your team ten yards farther away from the end zone. You call the ref (the smallest man on the field by at least fifty pounds) thirty-seven different names before you even think of calling the beloved offensive lineman who caused the penalty anything but your hero. That's the price you pay for putting on the black-and-white striped shirt every week during football season.

As Luckett Would Have It

Referees will often get the blame for a missed pass, a

holding penalty that didn't get called, or even for the weather being rotten. In almost all of these cases, the refs officiating the game remain more or less anonymous. The hatred and rancor don't get personal, and by Monday morning (Tuesday morning at the latest), everyone has moved on. This has not been the case with Phil Luckett. An NFL referee since 1991, Luckett, who officiated Super Bowl XXI, has had the misfortune of being involved in some very controversial plays and calls. One play in particular wasn't even a play, it was a coin toss. This "event" made Phil Luckett a household name for a few days and forced a microscope on his officiating that continues to this day. Every one of his close calls is questioned, and each time, the dreaded coin toss is mentioned. Does Luckett deserve the names and his fate, or is he a good ref with a bad rep? Here is the evidence:

Thanksgiving 1998, Detroit vs. Pittsburgh. Tied at 16 at the end of regulation. Sudden death. Referee Phil Luckett tosses the coin between the two teams' captains. Steelers' fullback Jerome Bettis calls "tails" before the coin hits the turf. The coin lands "tails." Luckett however, claims Bettis called "heads," and, after some heated arguments, gives the ball to the Lions, who drive down the field and kick a game-winning field goal.

Now, Luckett has always been blamed for this incident, even though when the NFL enhanced the tape of the coin toss, Bettis could be heard to have either said "hea-tails" or "head-tails." Even though a sideline microphone and camera picked up Bettis telling Steelers Bill Cowher that he said "hea-tails." Even though Detroit cornerback Robert Bailey heard differently. "To me, it sounded like one guy called heads and one guy called tails. That way, no matter what happens, you can argue. It's an old trick." Even though by rule, the first call during a coin toss is the one that stands. Sportscasters had a field day declaring that the Steelers had been robbed by an official, and Luckett's name has been associated with bad officiating since.

Thankfully, the NFL changed the coin-toss rule, decreeing that the call be made before the coin is tossed, but that hasn't helped Luckett any. In a profession where anonymity is a sign of success, Luckett's name has become synonymous with failure.

Of course, what happened ten days later didn't help his cause.

In the final minute of a game between the Jets and Seahawks, Jets quarterback Vinny Testaverde scored a touchdown on a fourth and goal quarterback sneak. Even though every camera angle showed that the ball never crossed the goal line, head linesman Ernie Frantz

I know, I know . . . referees are part of the playing field.

ruled Testaverde had scored. The Jets won the game and
Seattle, by extension, missed the playoffs. Who was the
head of the crew that day? Phil Luckett. Even though he
didn't make the call, he was held responsible. The NFL

quickly reinstated the use of instant replay for the 1999 season.

In December 2001, during a battle between the Saints and the Panthers, Saints quarterback Aaron Brooks and wide receiver Joe Horn executed a perfect flea-flicker at midfield, fooling the Panthers out of their pads. As Horn streaked down the field, Brooks threw a perfect pass that led Horn toward the goal line and right into an out-of-position Phil Luckett. The ball hit Luckett in the head as Horn ran him over. Pass incomplete. (Referees are considered part of the playing field.)

A good referee with a few lapses? A great referee who was in the wrong place at the wrong moment a couple of times? Or a poor referee rightfully vilified by fans and the press? Check out some of these plays on YouTube and decide for yourself.

Fifth Down and Goal to Go

Known as the Fifth Down Game, the 1990 contest between the Colorado Buffalos and their Big Eight Conference rivals the Missouri Tigers has been called one of the top moments (and blunders) in football history.

The twelfth ranked Buffs were down against the unranked Tigers 31-27 with less than three minutes to go. Deep in their own territory, backup quarterback, Charles Johnson led the Buffs down the field. With forty seconds to go, he completed a pass for a first down a few yards short of the goal line. On first down, Johnson spiked the ball to stop the clock. Second down, they were stopped just short of the goal line. Colorado then called a timeout, during which the officials *forgot to flip the down marker to note that it was now third down*. For third down, which was now second down, the Buffs were once again stopped from scoring. For fourth down, which was now third down, Johnson spiked the ball again, stopping the clock with two seconds left. Fourth down (really fifth down), Johnson tried a quarterback sneak, but was seemingly stopped short of the goal line. However, on a down that should have not been played, the officials signaled a touchdown that may or may not have been scored. Sure, heads rolled as the officials were suspended, but the score was upheld, and Colorado ended up winning the national title, despite needing a fifth down to win this one.

TOUGH TALK

Perhaps the survival of the fittest also applies to the loudest. Smashmouth football was once the province of the toughest, meanest, scariest players. The Butkuses and "Mean" Joe Greens of yesteryear made their living on physical aggressiveness. Today's top players need to put the media in their mean machines to stand out and set themselves apart. They still find their way inside the competition's head, but now do so with the help of twenty-four-hour sports coverage across every printed, broadcasted, and transmitted outlet conceivable. Once the worst things imaginable for a player was getting beat up on Sunday. Now there's the bonus of being shown up and then condemned to an eternal loop of YouTube clips rehashing it all.

A Word from our Sponsor

In the eighties, Bears quarterback Jim McMahon proved himself to be a product of the times in which he played. With his spiky hair and sunglasses (the latter he suggested were necessary after a childhood injury), McMahon was all arrogance and ego, with an arm strong enough to back it up. His brashness didn't endear him to the staff at BYU, who he felt failed to push hard enough for his Heisman consideration. He still broke or tied almost sixty NCAA Division I-A marks, was an All-American his senior year, and assuredly pushed the boundaries of the school's Mormon charter while he was there. As a pro, he regularly called out teammates, disregarded play calls, and yelled at coaches. By his own account, "Outrageousness is nothing more than a way to wake people up."

Living up to his own standard, McMahon woke up everyone within earshot. He stepped out of a limousine with a cold beer in hand at Halas Hall in Chicago to sign his first contact with the Bears. During Chicago's championship season in 1985, he developed a contusion on his butt. According to McMahon, it originated with his feet-first slides while keeping the ball (a practice he shied away from afterward), and it was only through the help of his acupuncturist that he could play. At the time, acupuncture was quite an "out there" concept for mainstream America, and in the week leading up to the Super Bowl, there was a media barrage of questions concerning his posterior. Fed up, or just looking for a fresh dose of outrage (he was already in the middle of another storm when a reporter falsely attributed to him condescending remarks aimed at the host city of New Orleans' women), McMahon gave the press hovering around the team's practice sessions an up-close and personal feature. As news helicopters flew overhead, McMahon dropped his pants and mooned them, making the source of his pain clear to all.

League commissioner Pete Rozelle was well aware of what kind of pain McMahon was. During the playoffs, Rozelle fined the QB $5,000 for breaking the league's uniform policy when his Adidas headband was clearly visible to the television cameras after he took off his helmet. During the NFC Championship game against the Rams, the commissioner and the country got a laugh the first time they saw McMahon's head. In place of his traditional Adidas gear was a new headband with "ROZELLE" written across the front. Rozelle found the stunt "funny as hell" and sent McMahon a personal note saying as much. McMahon may have gotten a laugh, but he didn't get his money back. It was funny, but it wasn't that funny.

Don't Lose My Number

Everyone's favorite complaint about professional football players involves the victory celebrations that follow even the smallest on-field accomplishments. Whether the players should just "play the game" or the "No Fun League" should lighten up, it's a part of the sport culture in an age of twenty-four-hour coverage and streaming highlights. Terrell Owens' infamous "Sharpie celebration" and Joe Horn's post TD cell phone call were either over-the-top arrogant or incredibly creative. (Owens pulled a Sharpie marker out of his sock and autographed a freshly caught touchdown ball to give to his agent during a 2002 San Francisco game against Seattle. Horn produced a cell phone hidden behind the goal post in a game against the Giants and called his kids.) Regardless of your take on either, at some point Chad Johnson's antics have taken the conversation to a new level—one worthy of a tip of the hat . . . or helmet.

Johnson's greatest hits include a preprinted sign addressing the NFL and requesting he not be fined for celebrating with the same preprinted sign. He once did an Irish step dance in the end zone, which would have been pretty ordinary by most standards unless you keep in mind that his Michael Flatley impersonation occurred in a game against the Bears. And that Chicago linebacker Brian Urlacher had just announced that his girlfriend—a Riverdance cast member—was pregnant. Johnson's routines became a story unto themselves, raising his popularity (and with it, the sales of his replica jerseys) and keeping the media guessing. He once fueled speculation that in honor of the Christmas season he would incorporate a live deer into a touchdown dance. (He didn't.) He was also featured in a *SportsCenter* commercial fielding ideas from the anchors as to what he should do next. What came next was the end of Chad Johnson and the rise of Ocho Cinco.

With number eighty-five on the back of his jersey, Johnson began referring to himself as "Ocho Cinco" in interviews, going so far as to have his new moniker taped to the back of his jersey. When league officials

Nice play honey. Now don't forget to pick up diapers after the game.

scoffed, Johnson did what any rational person would have done—he had his name legally changed. Chad Ocho Cinco began the 2008 season hoping to have Ocho Cinco jerseys fly off the shelves as he racked up catches for Cincinnati. Neither plan worked so well, as Ocho Cinco learned from the league's merchandising partner that their overstock of existing Johnson jerseys would keep them from creating a new one for him unless he was willing to spend millions buying up the lot. (He wasn't.) Worse for Bengals fans, his '08 season was lackluster at best, with injuries and a suspension costing him playing time and contributing to his lowest total receptions, yards, and touchdowns since his rookie year. While much credit goes to Ocho Cinco's wink-of-the-eye dance around league rules, it should be noted that all of his media savvy did nothing for his Spanish. The translation of "eighty-five" is not Ocho Cinco (which means 8-5), rather Ochenta Cinco. Whether it's Cinco, Johnson, or Mr. Ochenta, should his name ever be resolved on the back of his jersey, he better hope he doesn't get traded to the Lions, where Chuck Hughes' number eighty-five was retired in 2008.

He Lives for Trash

Trash talking has a certain psychological element. It can be an art form that seeks to take an opposing player out of his game. Or, in the case of Pittsburgh's Joey Porter, it can serve to energize the trash talker. Known for his 100-mile-per-hour rambling, Porter will go after anyone: the quarterback, the kicker, the ball boy. . . . In one game against the Tennessee Titans, Porter found himself on Tennessee's sidelines after a tackle. He started trying to trash talk his way out when one of the assistant coaches got so angry he threw a cup of hot coffee at Porter. The harder the target hits back, the harder Porter then comes after him during the game. And when Porter finally strikes a nerve, he knows he's won. He's been known to study opposing players' salaries, brushes with the law, and even domestic problems, and then use them in one of his monologues.

In 2003, Porter was shot while standing with friends outside a sports bar. He only missed two games, but it was a scary moment. And for a time, it altered his ability to trash talk. "They took my mean streak out of me," Porter said in an interview with ESPN.com. "They," being the well-wishers on opposing teams. "I can't sit there and get mad at this guy who just got done telling me, 'I was praying for you.'" Porter got his mojo back thanks to Rams tight end Brandon Manumaleuna, who said to Porter, "You're lucky it wasn't me, because I would have shot you in the face." Porter nearly took him out right then and there.

Taking Out the Trash

Trash talk is as much a part of the game as skinny kickers

and cheerleaders. Here is a random sampling of some of the more family-friendly trash talk stories:

The quarterback should be on the top of the list of players who just should NOT trash talk. No matter the score, the guys on the other end of the ball don't need extra provocation to want to kill you. Case and point: Ron Powlus, quarterback for Notre Dame (1994-1997) was enjoying a blowout against USC a little too much. Each time he approached the line he'd say, "This is our house! Get out of our house!" He was warned to stop several times, until finally he got hit so hard he had to leave for a down or two to take care of a split chin. He didn't say another word the rest of the game.

During a down-and-dirty, wet, mud pit of a game against the 49ers, a large mud ball flew into Chicago Bears linebacker Dick Butkus' eye as he was chasing a runner. The pain caused Butkus to lose consciousness, and there was some fear he might lose the eye. Thankfully, a doctor cleaned the eye, and Butkus seemed to be fine, especially after referee Norm Schachter called to him, "Thought you'd lost that eye. What would you do then?" Butkus hollered back, "I'd become a referee! One eye is more than I would need from what I've seen out here today."

In another battle of the wits between Schachter and Butkus, the ref penalized Butkus for roughing the passer. Butkus went nuts. Schachter let Butkus vent his . . . shall we call it . . . frustration, for a few downs. Finally Schachter said, "If you don't shut up, I'll bite your head off." "Go right ahead," Butkus replied. "Then you'll have more brains in your stomach than you do in your head."

Denver safety John Lynch (now with Tampa Bay), recounted this episode of mild trash talk: "One of

Just before losing consciousness, the quarterback made himself a promise: no more insulting linebackers' grandmothers.

our cornerbacks was covering Minnesota receiver Cris Carter. After one play Cris asked the guy how long he was in the league. He said, 'Three years.' Cris told him the NFL has a great dental plan and he should take advantage of it. The player just dropped to his knees laughing."

Stuff from the Locker Room

THERE may be no "I" in "T-E-A-M," but the individuals that pop up on any given roster are what give the game its character. The free spirits and oddballs who find a way to get the job done on the field, while softening the mental load carried by their teammates, are easier to relate to for most fans than the supermen who seem to be capable of nothing but the impossible. They humanize the action, and their stories rescue the game from a sea of stats and X and O diagrams.

ROLE PLAYERS

For the pranksters, jokesters, and one-of-a-kind characters, "creative" doesn't begin to describe the wilder side of the NFL and its more colorful players. The inmates may not run the asylum, but they definitely keep it interesting.

Gator Aid

Just because Larry Csonka is a hall of fame inductee and five-time Pro Bowler doesn't mean that the one-time Super Bowl MVP didn't get his hands dirty. In 1972, with the Dolphins' perfect regular season behind them and the Super Bowl approaching, Csonka realized he had a job to do. As New England would learn thirty-five years later, perfection without a championship only amounts to a footnote in the standings. Miami had lost the previous year's title game to Dallas, and Don Shula, the team's head coach, coached the Colts three years before that when they lost to the Jets in Super Bowl III. As a result, the mood around the team was tight.

During the week leading up to the big game, Csonka and teammate Manny Fernandez went fishing and caught a 3-foot baby alligator, and with it, an idea. The next day, while Coach Shula was meeting with the press, the two ran out to the parking lot, grabbed the gator, and placed it inside Shula's private shower. Hours later, as Shula disrobed and prepared to lather up, he found the baby gator waiting for him. The hall-of-fame coach ran out naked, past his secretary, and into the locker room to be met by his smiling players—proud of what they had accomplished. When he confronted them, Csonka immediately confessed, but added that Shula had, "won by one vote." When the coach inquired as to what he was talking about, Csonka informed him that by one vote he had won the right to tape the alligator's mouth shut. It was just enough silliness to break up the locker room and loosen everyone up for the game ahead.

Csonka and Fernandez weren't the only gator boosters in the NFL. A few years after Coach Shula's shower hijinks, Mike Barber of the Houston Oilers found a dead gator on the side of the road. Unlike the Dolphin

Has anyone seen my alligator shoes?

teammates, Barber could not take credit for breaking the tension of a championship club with what he was about to do. That said, for a brief moment, he could claim that he saved the lives of the team's defensive backs. He took the dead animal and threw it in a team meeting room where the backs were gathered to watch film. When he heard them yell out, he burst through the door and played the part of the hero.

Wardrobe Malfunction

Maybe Dan Dierdorf knew that some day his career would take him off the field and into the broadcast booth, and with that, he was compelled to help create good television whenever possible. A hall of famer and six-time Pro Bowler, Dierdorf was with the St. Louis Cardinals in 1975 when he took it upon himself to help teammate Conrad Dobler prepare for an interview. It wasn't just any interview, as it was going to be conducted by Phyllis George, a former beauty pageant winner. Dobler had a reputation as a dirty player, and in the face of such an attractive interviewer, he wanted to make the best impression he could possibly make. Dobler took an hour to prepare, laying out his clothes in the locker room and attending to various grooming practices previously neglected. While he wasn't looking, Dierdorf found the slacks Dobler had set aside, and proceeded to cut off one of the legs. When Dobler discovered the prank, he went ballistic, tearing up the room in search of either the culprit or substitute pants. The best he could find was tight end Jackie Smith, who offered Dobler a pair of his own. The problem was that Smith's pants were one size too small. Dobler had no choice but to suck it up in tight-end pants for his moment with Miss America.

Urban Cowboy

John Riggins walked out on the Jets in 1973, holding out for more money on his contract after being the team's first-round draft choice two years prior. When he returned, he did so wearing red leather pants, a feathered hat covering his Mohawk hairstyle, seated first on his motorcycle, and then on Coach Weeb Ewbank's desk as he signed his new contract. Holdouts and eccentric fashion were part of the price of admission for Riggins' talent as a running back. What his teams got was a Pro Bowler and future hall of famer who in 1982 led the league in rushing attempts, in 1983 led the league in touchdowns and rushing/receiving touchdowns, and also led the league in rushing touchdowns in both 1983 and 1984.

Riggins' on-field performance was crucial to the Redskins, his on-and-off team from 1976 through the end of his career. (The "off" periods being those of semiretirement and a contract holdout.) In 1982, his 43-yard touchdown run against Miami broke open Super Bowl XVII. Off the field, as a Washington, DC sports star, he played to a different audience. Once, at a black-tie function at the National Press Club, he found himself seated across from Sandra Day O'Connor. "C'mon Sandy baby," he told the Supreme Court Justice. "Loosen up, you're too tight." Shortly after, he passed out and napped on the floor while then-Vice President George H.W. Bush addressed the room. Riggins was escorted out by security. Like his teammates, who occasionally put up with nonsense only to reap rewards, Justice O'Connor was the recipient of a dozen roses as an apology from Riggins. Of course, history could have taken an odd turn had he sent her a pair of her own red leather pants, instead.

Candy Bowl

Joe Montana to Jerry Rice made for one of the most successful throwing/receiving tandems in NFL history (with Steve Young to Rice a legitimate challenger, depending on whether you value regular or postseason performance). When asked about his passing partner, Rice wastes no time selling Montana out as a prankster. "Joe Montana did crazy things," Rice said about the Hall-of-Fame QB. "He would put Tiger Balm and stuff like that in jocks. Then all of a sudden guys would put their jocks on and they'd get that little burning sensation out there on the field!"

Despite the hot pants treatment, it was Montana's coolness in the huddle with the game on the line that earned him his reputation and the nickname Joe Cool. Perhaps the best example of poise under fire took place during Super Bowl XXIII, with the 49ers down three with 3:20 left in the game. With the championship on the line, Montana stood in the huddle during a TV timeout, turned to his teammates, and said, "There, in

Joe Cool had the ability to keep his team hot.

the stands, standing near the exit ramp . . . isn't that John Candy?" After spotting the comedian in the crowd, he drove the team ninety-two yards down the field and threw the winning touchdown with :30 left.

All About Clinton

Clinton Portis is a man of character—dozens actually.

In 2005, following two consecutive Redskin losses, Portis showed up for the team's weekly Thursday press conference not quite himself. The running back had donned a white wig and a pair of skinny, visor-like sunglasses, and claimed that he had stuck his hand in a socket that morning and was now "the Mad Scientist," on a mission to dissect the playbook to figure out how he could reach the end zone. A week later, Portis showed up in a black wig, Lone Ranger mask, black cape, yellow sunglasses, and gold teeth, calling himself Southeast Jerome.

Portis continued the parade of personas, bringing around the likes of Dr. I Don't Know (who regrettably informed the media of the passing of Southeast Jerome, the victim of a holdup during an illegal poker game with

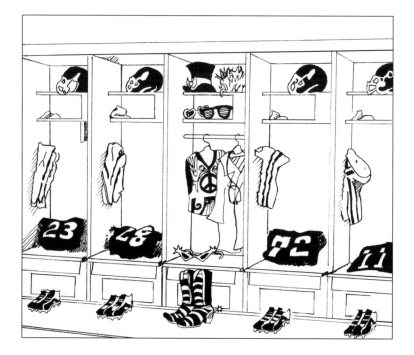

Okay, who's got my wig? Not the black one, but the purple one with the glitter. Come on guys, the press conference is in five minutes and I NEED MY WIG!

Yankee third baseman Alex Rodriguez), Sheriff Gonna Getcha, Inspector 2-2 (who were both investigating the death of Southeast Jerome and seeking persons of interest, specifically the Barber brothers, Ronde and Tiki), and Dolla Bill (Southeast Jerome's purple-haired employer, also involved in the manhunt search for Jerome's killer, with a personal stake as Jerome owed him money).

The cast of characters expanded to include Reverend Gonna Change (brought in to change Washington's luck—the team was 5-6 when he arrived and then won five in a row to make the playoffs), Coach Janky Spanky (who suggested an extra two defenders might work best in stopping Portis' game), and eventually, the Angel of Southeast Jerome himself (hanging with his homies up in heaven). The cavalcade rolled for several years, and while the combined wisdom of Coconut Jones, Dolomite Jenkins, Choo Choo (the team dance instructor), or Dr. Do Itch Big failed to shine further light on the identity of Southeast Jerome's killer, there's always someone else around the corner.

SMELLS LIKE TEAM SPIRIT

Not every team has a standout personality on the bench waiting to leave teammates and adversaries alike scratching their heads. Sometimes it's a single play, or a ritual that breaks up the monotony of a weekly schedule. Sometimes everything is as it always is until your coach drops his drawers in the locker room.

Practice Makes Perfect

The original Dallas Texans emerged out of the ashes of the defunct All-American Football Conference's New York Yankees (no relation to the baseball franchise). The team's run in the NFL was brief, as they were eventually sold back to the league and reborn (again) when Carol Rosenbloom bought them for Baltimore, returning the Colts to the city and its devoted fans. (Baltimore had lost its AAFC club in 1950 after only one season in the NFL.) Jeff Davis recounts the early days of the Dallas club in *Rozelle*, his thorough biography of Commissioner Pete Rozelle. One story (told to him by former Rozelle assistant Ernie Accorsi) makes it obvious why the early Dallas team was destined for failure.

The Texans were not the fan favorites that their regional descendents, the Cowboys, proved to be, with the combined attendance of their first four home games at the Cotton Bowl unable to generate the equivalent of a single sellout. To increase revenue, they became a road team, operating out of Hershey, Pennsylvania. With a game on the schedule against Philadelphia, and the two

But coach, you gotta see these guys. They can spike serve!

teams now close in proximity to each other, Eagles head coach Jim Trimble instructed fullback John Hufzar to skip practice, spy on the Texans, and write down what plays they were practicing. Hufzar took his spy role seriously, hiding out in a parked car near where the vagabond Dallas team was supposed to be preparing for Sunday's game, wearing dark sunglasses and a cap pulled down low to hide his face as he scouted the opposition. When he called Trimble that night to inform his coach what to expect come Sunday, he had little to report.

"What'd they do?" Trimble asked. "They played volleyball across the crossbar of the goalpost," Hufzar informed him. "What else?" Trimble prompted. Hufzar had nothing.

Instructed to stay another night to hopefully learn more, Hufzar called his coach again the next day. "Coach, they're still playing volleyball," Hufzar said. Philadelphia won the game 38-21.

Swimming Against the Current

In 1964, the Vikings were playing the 49ers and up

27-17 in the fourth quarter. With the ball on their own 34-yard line, San Francisco halfback Billy Kilmer fumbled. Defensive end Jim Marshall recovered and ran sixty-six yards to freedom. Without a single San Francisco player impeding his progress, Marshall crossed the goal line, and to celebrate, he tossed the ball out of the end zone and toward the fans.

He expected to be greeted by his defensive corps to help him celebrate the turnover and the six points of insurance he had secured for Minnesota. Instead, 49ers center Bruce Bosley came over and congratulated him. The scoreboard read 27-19, not 33-17. Also, there was no kicking team coming over from the Minnesota bench to attempt the extra point.

Jim Marshall had run the wrong way. Worse than that, he had run thirty-four yards farther to score points for the other team than he would have needed to get the touchdown for the Vikings. Had he simply crossed the goal line, it would have been a touchback and Minnesota would have gotten the ball at their own 20, but because he spiked it out the back of the end zone, San Francisco was awarded two points for the safety.

Twice in his career, Jim Marshall was selected to the Pro Bowl. The defensive end led the league in fumble returns in 1963, in safeties in 1968, and in 1964 was the league leader in trips to the end zone that the rest of his team was defending.

More "Current" Events

During the 1929 Rose Bowl, California's Roy Riegels snatched up a fumble by Georgia Tech's Stumpy Thomason. Unfortunately, Riegels had gotten turned around during the play and was running toward his own end zone. His speedy teammate Benny Lom tried to stop

Other way, stupid!

him, but Riegels yelled, "Get away from me! This is my touchdown!" Lom finally got Riegels to pull up at the 3-yard line, where most of Tech's players tackled them at the 1. Cal chose to punt rather than risk a play so close to their own end zone, but Tech's Vance Maree blocked Lom's punt and Georgia Tech scored a safety, giving them a 2-0 lead.

Riegels was so distraught that he had to be talked into returning to the game. Lom passed for a touchdown and kicked the extra point, and Riegels blocked a Tech punt in the second half, but Tech won the game by a final score of 8-7. Riegels, who became "Wrong Way" Riegels, eventually had a sense of humor about the whole thing and even capitalized on the blunder by parodying his famous run in vaudeville acts. He also reportedly later sent Jim Marshall (see previous story) a letter reading, "Welcome to the club."

That's all folks!

Shooting for the Moon

Former first-round draft pick and hall-of-fame line-backer Mike Singletary had a reputation as a team leader during his playing days. According to his coach, an impromptu motivational speech by the Bears' captain had his teammates fired up and throwing furniture by the time he was done talking. Of course, for his fellow players, following a ten-time Pro-Bowler and two-time NFL Defensive Player of the Year was something of a no-brainer. As head coach of the San Francisco 49ers, Singletary didn't have the luxury of weekly big hits and on-field feats to remind his players of who they were dealing with. That's not to say he didn't know how to show them who was boss.

In his first game on the job, down 20-3 at the half to the Seahawks during the 2008 season, Singletary needed to make it clear how his team's play up to that point made him feel. He needed to get their attention and spark their competitive spirit. So he took off his pants.

While coaching in one's boxers is a unique technique, it wasn't enough to get San Fran over the hump, as it

Brief discussion with the ref.

only netted the team a touchdown and a field goal—
not enough to overtake Seattle's 34-point performance.
It's possible that the final deficit was the result of some
players not getting the message (locker rooms do get

crowded after all and not everyone gets a front-row seat for their pantless coach). Tight end Vernon Davis, for example, was called for an egregious fourth-quarter penalty, and then shrugged off his fully-dressed coach's attempt to discuss the situation. Preferring to avoid a wardrobe malfunction on live television, Singletary opted to throw Davis out of the game, politely suggesting he sit in the stands and watch from there instead. Following the 34-13 loss, he apologized to the fans forced to witness such ugliness. It's unclear whether he was referring to the game or the possibility that season-ticket packages included locker room passes.

Hazing the Titans

Sports and hazing go hand in hand. Ask any junior varsity athlete after a long practice followed by a run-in with the varsity squad. It's nature's way of maintaining the pecking order, if nature were privy to public nudity, women's clothing, manual labor, and other acts meant to demean its participants. Hotshot rookies need to be reminded that the game was not created on the day they made their first appearance as a starter, and if it takes shaving cream and toilet paper to bring that message home, so be it.

Regardless of the sport, things are no different at the professional level. The Tennessee Titans maintain order through a dizzy bat race, where rookies put their foreheads to a baseball bat and are then spun around until they can't tell up from down and left from right, and are then forced to attempt to proceed in a straight line. Such advancement requires healthy legs, and injured rookies, having escaped the brutal regimen of training camp, cannot be expected to participate.

During the summer of 2008, veteran Keith Bulluck

So, you rookies think you're hot stuff, eh?

targeted injured rookies Lavelle Hawkins and Cary Williams, and tied them to a goal post. Afterward, Bulluck, along with his teammates Albert Haynesworth and Rob Bironas, proceeded to prepare a worthwhile lunch for the young players to assist in their convalescence. Specifically, the vets doused Tennessee's next generation with water, mustard, ketchup, flour, and anything else they could get their hands on. While a free lunch is the sort of thing that usually keeps a growing football player happy, Hawkins did complain at one point that he couldn't breathe. Teammate Jason Murphy turned to the receiver and asked, "Then how are you talking?"

The wisdom of the elders is not to be disputed, especially while tied to a pole.

Stuff Without a Helmet

FOOTBALL has been said to be more than just a contact game, but rather a "collision sport," bringing together forces from every direction, seen and unseen. Plays go from by the book to adlibbed without warning, and when they do, what follows is usually what keeps us coming back each and every Sunday (Saturday if you're a fan of college ball, Friday if it's the high school game that keeps you going). No other sport attempts to adhere so regularly to its own script. And with each side calling in the action for each down, sooner or later something's gonna give. On and off the field, some of the oddest moments and characters find their way into the spotlight as soon as things stop going according to plan.

WHAT JUST HAPPENED?

It's a good thing football has embraced instant replay, as

every now and then, the action on the field takes an unexpected turn, leaving those watching in the stands and at home wondering if they just saw what they thought they saw. Whether it's Ohio State coach Woody Hayes punching Clemson noseguard Charlie Bauman after an interception during the 1978 Orange Bowl, or the final minutes of a pivotal matchup between the Raiders and the Jets (including an Oakland comeback) being pulled from the air in favor of a special network presentation of *Heidi*, the unexpected happens, and it's what keeps playbooks as thick as they are. You can plan for every contingency, but there are Shirley Temple-sized forces of nature that simply can't be stopped, and once they've had their way, the rest of us are left scratching our heads.

Day Tripper

In 1957, during the CFL Championship game between

the Winnipeg Blue Bombers and the Hamilton Tiger-Cats, the Bombers were getting blown out. With the score already out of hand at 32-7, there was nothing Winnipeg or their fans could do to stop the carnage . . . almost nothing.

David Humphrey had no ticket to the big game. Then a defense attorney, he knew most of the cops working the security detail at Varsity Stadium in Toronto, and eventually found himself standing on the Bombers' sideline with the team, watching the action. He had also had a bit to drink. When Hamilton defensive back Ray Bawel intercepted a Winnipeg pass and was on his way to run up the score even further, the crowd in attendance saw the beret-clad fan step forward and trip Bawel on his return. Afterward, Humphrey returned briefly to the Winnipeg sideline before making his way around the field to the Ticat area, searching for Bawel

Have a nice trip. See you next fall.

and a fight. When the player was nowhere to be found, Humphrey grabbed a chair from the Hamilton sideline. He was stopped by security, who promptly let him go when they recognized him from the game.

Beyond the amused fans in Toronto, there was also a national television audience watching at home as well (a relative novelty at this point in CFL history), and suddenly the world had gotten so small that the drunken exploits of a single football fan, which would have previously faded with the next morning's hangover, were now part of a countrywide conversation. He was "The Tripper." For his own sake, Humphrey was fortunate enough to keep his name out of the story. Fifty years later, Humphrey is a Superior Court Judge who has finally owned up to his youthful discretions. He also freely admits that if he had been presented with the facts of his own case, he would have found himself guilty. Perhaps to ease his own conscious, he did reach out and attempt to make amends with Bawel. He gave the former Hamilton player a watch with the inscription "Grey Cup 1957 from The Tripper." When, at age eighty-two, he was invited to the Rogers Centre with his son to celebrate the anniversary of his famous trip, his son told officials, "Don't worry about my dad, we'll make sure someone always has a hold of him so he won't go wandering off."

Cookies, Milk, and Boos for Santa

If Eagles fans had known that Donovan McNabb would be the first quarterback to lead the team to a Super Bowl since Ron Jaworski did so in 1980, it probably wouldn't have stopped them from booing him when Philly selected the Syracuse grad with their first pick (second overall) in the 1999 draft. (The citizens of brotherly love had their eyes on Rickie Williams, who, in turn, had his eyes on quitting football to pursue higher grounds a few years later.) McNabb was admittedly annoyed by their reaction, but considering the history of the franchise and its fan base, he should have considered himself in good company.

Thirty years prior, the Eagles sat at 2-11 on the last day of the 1968 season, hosting Minnesota. The second of the two wins had removed any chance of the Eagles getting the top pick in the following year's draft (which went to Buffalo, giving the Bills a promising running back with anger issues out of USC named O.J. Simpson). With snow on the ground and in the seats from the night before, the 20°F weather at Franklin Field was intensified by thirty-mile-per-hour wind gusts. Regardless of the weather, 55,000 Philadelphia fans came out to support their team, knowing that there was nothing on the line, nothing to look forward to, and no comfort to be found in the conditions.

A 7-0 Philly lead was erased just before the half, thanks to a Minnesota interception and a 57-yard touchdown pass. Fortunately, halftime promised a treat for the fans. The Eagles cheerleaders had dressed like scantily-clad elves, and Santa was scheduled to make an appearance—accompanied by a marching band playing Christmas songs. Unfortunately, the snow and mud made the field too soggy for the float that had been set to carry Santa around the field, so he would have to walk. Even worse, the man in red was nowhere to be found. (Some say he got stuck in traffic, while others suggest that Rudolph wasn't the only red-nosed icon that night.)

Quick-thinking Eagles entertainment director Bill Mullen plucked twenty-year old Frank Olivo, already dressed in red with a fake white beard, out of the stands and had him fill in. Perhaps it was the score, or a collective outrage over the insult-added-to-injury appearance of a scrawny unSanta-like Santa that drove the crowd to its breaking point. It might have been years of building fan frustration with management coming to a boiling point.

Either way, Philadelphia's heart shrunk three times that day, and they took their rage out on old Saint Nick. The boos began raining on Olivo as soon as he stepped on to the field. They were followed by a few snowballs heaved from the upper deck. Then a few more. Soon, hundreds of Eagles fans had Santa in their crosshairs, each finding their target better than any Philadelphia quarterback had done all season.

Thirty years later, Olivo stepped back into the red suit as part of a 76ers promotion. With no safe place for Santa in Philly, he was promptly booed. At least he could be thankful that basketball is an indoor sport, and boos are all that rained down on him this time.

The Nose Tackle's Meow

Jim Burt spent the bulk of his career as a nose tackle for the New York Giants. By the time he moved on to San Francisco in 1989, he already had a Pro Bowl appearance and a Super Bowl ring to his credit, but only a limited number of starts to look forward to in the Bay area over his final three seasons. As a 49er, Burt had annual rematches with his old team on the schedule, and was sought after for scouting advice as to the best way to get past his former mates. Always a team player, Burt let on about the irrational fear of cats that one of the Giants' linemen suffered from.

When the two teams met face-to-face, the 49er players were ready. Prior to each snap, the San Francisco defense would make cat noises from the line of scrimmage, hoping to spook and distract their New York counterparts. When the tactic seemed to have no effect, the

49ers tried harder, incessantly meowing with each play.

The pangs of anxiety that typically surface when facing the object of one's fear were never felt on the playing field that day. Ailurophobia (the fear of cats) was not even on the active roster. No Giant player feared cats, kittens, or any other type of feline, although there was a group of offensive linemen more than a little puzzled as to why the 49ers sounded like a back alley full of strays on the prowl. Burt had made it all up, getting a laugh at the expense of both his old team and his new team at the same time. Perhaps he thought they were a bunch of pussycats—the Giants soft for not retaining his services and the 49ers for asking him to give up his old teammates.

Spiked Punch to the Gut

The history of the New York Jets after Joe Namath led

them to victory in Super Bowl III has been far from illustrious. In the twenty-five years following Namath's guarantee, Gang Green has only seen the playoffs five times, with their best run a loss to the Dolphins in the 1982 AFC Championship Game.

The 1994 team had a shot at finally turning the corner. Only three years removed from their last post-season effort (a Wild Card loss to the Oilers), New York had a 6-5 record in November, with a shot at their share of first place thanks to a late-November matchup with Miami, who was sitting on top of the division at 7-4.

Before a record Giants Stadium crowd (for a Jets game), New York jumped ahead 17-0. With four minutes to go in the third quarter they led 24-6 before hall-of-fame quarterback Dan Marino took over the game, and the division. Fifteen unanswered points off Marino's arm (and Mark Ingram's hands) brought the Dolphins within reach at 24-21. With 2:34 remaining, Miami began a drive at their own 16-yard line and marched down the field. A Marino completion to New York's 8-yard line with the clock running down had the Dolphins scrambling to the line of scrimmage, their quarterback yelling, "Clock! Clock! Clock!" as he ordered his team to formation. The ball was hiked and Marino made a spiking motion, selling the play that backup quarterback Bernie Kosar had brought to the team, and the Jets bought it. Convinced that Miami was stopping the clock, rookie cornerback Aaron Glenn got caught sleeping and held up on his coverage. Marino held on to the ball, turned, and fired a laser into the end zone to Ingram for their fourth touchdown hookup. 28-24, final.

The fake spike was to become the stuff of legends, as it not only completed the comeback, and dashed New

York's shot at first place, but did so with agonizing style. The Jets never recovered, losing the remainder of the games on their 1994 schedule and finishing the season at 6-10. From the fake spike forward, the Jets would go 4-32 with nothing resembling the playoffs in their sites until Bill Parcells took over in 1997, leading them to the '98 AFC Championship (where they lost to Denver).

Grilled Mascot in Lemon Sauce

How proud the University of Texas was to debut their new mascot, a real, live, longhorn steer, on Thanksgiving Day, 1916. The animal even inspired the Longhorns to a spirited victory against their arch rivals, Texas A&M. Bevo, as he soon became known, was in a pretty awful mood though and charged a photographer—probably because Bevo was shipped to the school by train without any food or water. Things only went downhill from there. Bevo was soon secretly branded (most likely by some Aggies) with "13-0," which was the score the Longhorns had recently lost to the Aggies by. Later, Bevo was shipped off to a ranch, where he remained until 1920, when he became dinner for the Longhorn's annual football banquet. (You can only hope they treated their cheerleaders better than that.)

Bevo's spirit, however, lived on. Bevo II once charged an SMU cheerleader, who had to fight off the steer with his megaphone. Bevo III escaped his enclosure and ran around the campus for two days. Bevo IV attacked a car. Most of the subsequent Bevo mascots have been tamer, and today, the Texas longhorn steer is one of the most recognized college mascots. The shape of his horns even gave rise to the school's hand symbol. According to some, the "Hook 'em Horns" is also a satanic salute or a cheerful way to signal "Rock on!"

OFF THE GRIDIRON

Not every football head scratcher happens on the field. The business of football, and the media coverage it generates, is a spectacle on to itself. With around-the-clock television coverage, call-in radio shows, and open response forums on websites everywhere, football and the off-the-field dramas of its players make for a never-ending reality television marathon, complete with scandal, theatrics, and the occasional laughing stock who literally shoots himself in the leg (and his team in the foot).

Dollar League

When the AFL came on the scene to challenge the NFL, it was only a matter of time before the two leagues merged. Not that the merger was inevitable from day one, but once the new league proved viable, it made the most sense. In the eighties, perhaps the USFL and its founders thought that, as a budding league, they, too, were on a similar trek. Headed by former CEO and founding president of ESPN, Chet Simmons, the new league played a spring schedule with what were, at the time, innovative rule changes (two-point conversions and instant replay) and began to develop a following. As with the AFL a generation prior, the USFL tossed money at top college stars to draw key talent away from the NFL. Herschel Walker signed a record contract, and New Jersey Generals owner Donald Trump made a million-dollar bid to woo iconic coach Don Shula as well. (Shula turned it down after talks of their negotiation were leaked to the press.) When a fall schedule was announced, signifying direct competition with the established league, it was only a matter of time before things came to a head.

The NFL vs. the USFL went to the courts as an antitrust suit in 1984. The case against the established league was that it went out of its way to stifle their rivals. Things got ugly as accusations flew, especially when rogue owner Al Davis testified against his peers. When the case was handed over to a jury to decide, it didn't take them long to come back with a verdict against the NFL.

It was a seemingly devastating blow, turned on its head moments later when the damages were declared. To the plaintiff, the USFL, the amount of $1. The final check, totaling $3.76 (accounting for interest and full damages) remains un-cashed to this day.

Hold the Cheesesteak

Warren Sapp had a reputation for having a big mouth. From 1995-2007, the defensive tackle ate up the opposition, averaging over thirty tackles a season with nearly one hundred quarterback sacks. Off the field, Sapp had to be a little more careful with his diet, especially as a visiting player. As a Buccaneer, Sapp claimed that while on the road, his food was poisoned on multiple occasions by overzealous fans. The notion that crazed fans would try to keep a player from getting in a big game was widespread. Sapp's teammate at the time Keenan McCardell recalled the instructions of Super Bowl-winning coach Tom Coughlin, then with Jacksonville, who told his players, "Don't eat anything outside of what we're served as a team."

According to Sapp, his food was tampered with at least twice during the season and once during the playoffs. One incident occurred in Philadelphia as the Bucs were preparing to meet the Eagles in 2002, on the road to an eventual victory in Super Bowl XXXVII. The other followed the team's championship victory over the Oakland Raiders. Sapp and a friend were back in Philadelphia and stopped for dinner en route to Madison Square Garden to see Michael Jordan play against the Knicks. Sapp made his friend swap meals with him, and the friend spent the entire drive to New York getting sick as a result. Sapp learned his lesson, insisting on water from sealed bottles and even going so far as to book multiple rooms during road trips—one under his name and one for an alias, which he used to order room service. Fortunately for Sapp, after leaving Tampa Bay for Oakland, the only thing that had the potential to induce vomiting was the Raiders' record, as the team averaged fewer than four wins a season while he was there.

Roughing the Sacker

Michael Strahan's relationship with the media throughout his career was tempestuous at best. The Giants Pro Bowl defensive end and single-season sack leader has never shied away from speaking his mind, and it came as no surprise in 2006 to viewers of *Best Damn Sports Show Period*, a cable sports roundup, that he would call out co-host Tom Arnold for things he had reportedly written about Strahan in his upcoming book. What might have surprised some was the brawl that ensued, as the 300-pound backfield terror took on the sitcom player and occasional actor. Most shocking was that after the fight, it was Strahan, not Arnold, calling out in pain—not since Tyson-Douglas had an underdog of such magnitude been the last man standing after a faceoff.

Of course, careful observers would have recalled that Tom Arnold didn't have a new book scheduled for publication at the time. They would have also noted the

You thought you were tough!

calendar—sitting on the first day of April. Then those same careful observers would have remembered what Michael Strahan did for a living. As a large, ferocious man responsible for knocking others down, the only explanation for his fall to Arnold was that the fix was in. An April Fool's joke on both the show's co-hosts (including Ron Dibble, Chris Rose, and Rodney Peete, who helped break up "the fight") and Giants fans (Giants' head coach Tom Coughlin and owner Wellington Mara were informed of the shenanigans ahead of time).

The Vagabond Halfback

Johnny "Blood" McNally, a charter member of the Hall of Fame, played for several NFL teams in the '20s and '30s, including the Duluth Eskimos, Milwaukee Badgers, Pottsville Maroons, and Pittsburgh Pirates (and Steelers). It was with the Green Bay Packers, however, that Johnny Blood was at his peak . . . both on *and* off the field. Known back then as a "rakish, colorful, free spirit," today's paparazzi-induced media would have loved Blood, who, in modern lingo would have been called a womanizer and a drunk. Not only was Blood known for his speed, elusiveness, and play-making ability, but also for his inability to follow rules. Once called "a Peter Pan who would never shed his eternal youth," Blood broke as many curfews as he did football records. In fact, his life and career are the basis for the character Dodge Connolly in the movie *Leatherheads*, with George Clooney playing the title role.

Here are just a few of his fabled exploits.

- Once, while playing for the Duluth Eskimos, the team's owner found the well-read but intoxicated Blood out past curfew reciting poetry on a street corner. He locked Blood in his sixth-floor hotel room. But Blood escaped out the window, dropped down onto the window ledge one floor down, and knocked on the window. By the time the team owner returned to his room, he found Blood reciting poetry to his girlfriend.

- Called the "Vagabond Halfback" after once getting caught returning to Green Bay by traveling in a train's baggage compartment, Blood once missed the team's train as they headed out for an away game. Undeterred, he, along with a woman friend (the reason for his lateness), drove his car ahead of the train and parked it on the tracks to await the train. He and his girlfriend stayed in the car while the train screeched to a halt. Then, Blood got out of the car and onto the train as his friend drove off.

- During Green Bay's run for the 1930 championship, quarterback Red Dunn threw a pass in the flat to Blood for a long score. A few games later, Dunn attempted the same play, only to have Blood lateral it back to him. Dunn was quickly tackled for a loss. Blood later told Dunn that he just wanted to see what he would do with the ball.

- In 1930, while the Packers were returning home by train after winning the 1930 championship, Blood decided to tease a teammate by throwing wet napkins at him. After asking Blood to stop several times, the much bigger and stronger Lavie Dilweg stood up and chased Blood down the aisles until they both reached the last compartment. Thinking he had Blood cornered, Dilweg yelled triumphantly, only to watch helplessly as Johnny went out onto the back railing and climbed to the roof of the train. He then ran back toward the front of the train, jumping from car to car, until he reached

Next stop, Crunch Town!

the safety of the engineer's cab, where they enjoyed a friendly conversation until the train pulled into the station.

- The next year, Curly Lambeau, Green Bay's coach, withheld most of Blood's pay throughout the season in order to keep him sober. Blood had his greatest year, scoring fourteen touchdowns and leading Green Bay to their third straight championship.

Do you think either of the Manning brothers could get away with any of this?

Under an Assumed Name

Every now and then, the NFL is forced to ban certain customized jerseys from its licensed shops. The banned list includes obscenities, inappropriate language, and some made-up names and number combinations.

In 2008, one name/number combination needed to

be quickly banished. The newest member of the banned laundry society was the #17 New York Giants jersey personalized with "H. Smith" on the back. Harris Smith happened to be the name wide receiver Plaxico Burress used to check himself into the hospital after accidentally shooting himself in the thigh when his gun slipped free from his sweatpants while out at a New York nightclub. Plaxico's accident (coining the term "plaxident") cost him millions and eventually got him cut from the team. As of this writing, he still faces criminal charges and eternal mockery.

RANDOM HITS

Although the long bomb into the end zone is a great spectacle, sometimes it's the little outlet passes and short runs that get you the six points on the board. In honor of the three- and four-yard gains, the *Book of Football Stuff* concludes with some unforgettable football shorts.

He Said What?

FSU Seminoles coach Bill Peterson was once asked by a reporter whether he thought it would rain on game day. Peterson replied, "What do you think I am, a geologist?"

Joe Jacoby, an offensive tackle for the Washington Redskins once said that he would run over his own mother to win the Super Bowl. "To win the Super Bowl," the Oakland Raiders' Matt Millen replied, "I'd run over Joe's mom, too!"

During an interview one day, Minnesota Vikings kicker Gary Anderson was asked how much he could bench press. Not much, apparently. Anderson confessed that he did not even know where the weight room was.

Michael Vick, the former Atlanta Falcon's QB once

said, "I have two weapons—my legs, my arm, and my brains." ABC Radio's Keith Olbermann later replied, "Mike didn't say they were sharp weapons."

The normally modest Jerry Rice once said to reporters, "I feel like I'm the best, but you're not going to get me to say that."

Joe Theismann said that, "Nobody in football should be called a genius. A genius is a guy like Norman Einstein."

Head coach Bruce Coslet on his 1997 Bengals: "We can't run. We can't pass. We can't stop the run. We can't stop the pass. We can't kick. Other than that, we're just not a very good football team right now."

Bo Jackson on his competition: "If my mother put on a helmet and shoulder pads and a uniform that wasn't the same as the one I was wearing, I'd run over her if she was in my way. And I love my mother."

I love you, too, son, but momma's gonna lay you flat.

Testing Your Luck

Gary Anderson, the Minnesota Viking's placekicker in 1998, converted all thirty-five of his attempted field goals and all fifty-nine extra points in the regular season—becoming the first placekicker to do so. However, his one miss during the playoffs came during the NFC Championship Game against the Falcons. The miss gave the Falcons a chance to come back and win the game.

Before the 1940 NFL Championship Game, Redskins owner George Marshall told reporters that he thought the Bears were crybabies and quitters when the going got tough after a 7-3 loss to his Skins a few weeks earlier. Chicago head coach, George Halas, showed his team the article as a motivational tool. Final score? Chicago 73, Washington 0.

Top-ranked Boston College had won their first eight games in 1942, and needed one more win (against the mediocre Holy Cross Crusaders) to clinch their undefeated season and a trip to the Sugar Bowl. Unfortunately, they scheduled and planned the victory party at a hot nightspot before the game . . . and lost miserably in a 55-12 rout. While this game is still remembered as one of the most amazing upsets in college football history, what happened next put the game into perspective. After the loss, BC cancelled the party, and that night, the nightclub burned to the ground. It remains the second most deadly building fire in American history.

Overrated

Sure Joe Namath played an amazing game to win Super Bowl III against the heavily favored Baltimore Colts, but he wasn't a particularly good quarterback even if he is in the Hall of Fame. During his career he threw 220 interceptions versus 173 touchdowns, and after the famous Super Bowl victory, he only won two games against winning teams for the remaining eight years of his career.

In 1989, the Minnesota Vikings traded five players

and six draft picks to the Dallas Cowboys for superstar Herschel Walker. The draft picks (Dallas picked up Emmitt Smith, Darren Woodson, and Kevin Smith) helped the Cowboys build up to three Super Bowl victories in the '90s. The Vikings won the NFC Central in 1989, but lost in the playoffs and were in last place a year later. Walker played for the Vikings for two and a half years, never running for more than 1,000 yards in a season. Soon after, he competed in the 1992 Winter Olympics in the two-man bobsled.

Curiosities

Due to the Second World War, NFL football clubs had trouble fielding teams. In 1943, Pittsburgh and Philadelphia had a novel solution: They combined clubs and called themselves the Steagles. The following year, Pittsburgh teamed up with the Chicago Cardinals, and the

That tall guy hit me hard.

team became known as the Carpets (Card-Pitt).

The Baltimore Colts had just lost to the Pittsburgh Steelers in the 1976 playoffs when a Colt fan crashed his small plane into the upper deck of Memorial Stadium. No one was hurt, but it was a fitting end for a season that had suddenly gone up in flames for Baltimore.

In the first part of the twentieth century, the Bears' fierce, 235-pound running back, Bronko Nagurski, was so strong that he often broke opposing players' bones and left tackles unconscious. His style was to run straight ahead and knock over anyone or anything that got in the way. Once he inadvertently ran into a mounted police officer who was patrolling behind the end zone. Nagurski hit the horse, knocking it in the air before it crashed to the ground. Incredibly, no one—not even Nagurski—was hurt.

In 1966, the AFL and NFL decided to merge, with

Wow, coach really *dressed him down.*

the winner of each new division to meet in what NFL Commissioner Pete Rozelle wanted to call "The Big One." During discussions, Kansas City Chiefs owner Lamar Hunt jokingly suggested calling it "The Super Bowl" after one of his children's favorite toys, a Super Ball. The ball can be viewed at the Pro Football Hall of Fame.

As punishment for goofing off during practice, Chicago Bears coach George Halas ordered defensive end Doug Atkins to run a lap of the field with his helmet on. Atkins took the coach at his word and ran the lap wearing his helmet—and nothing else.

References

Books

Conner, Floyd. *Football's Most Wanted: The Top Book of the Great Game's Outrageous Characters, Fortunate Fumbles, and Other Oddities.* Potomac Books Inc., 2000.

Davis, Jeff. *Rozelle: Czar of the NFL.* McGraw-Hill, 2007.

Huizenga, Rob. *You're Okay, It's Just a Bruise.* Macmillan, 1995.

Rand, Jonathan. *300 Pounds of Attitude: The Wildest Stories and Craziest Characters the NFL Has Ever Seen.* The Lyons Press, 2007.

Tally, Steve. *Almost America: From the Colonists to Clinton: a "WHAT IF" History of the U.S.* Harper Collins, 2000.

Taylor, Lawrence. *LT: Over the Edge: Tackling Quarter-*

backs, Drugs, and a World Beyond Football. HarperTorch, 2004.

Newspapers and Web Articles

Gay, Nancy. "Singletary dropped pants at halftime," www.sfgate.com, October 31, 2008.

Heller, Dick. "The way it was," The Washington Times; January 12, 2009.

Lord, Rich. "Mayor wants to drop 'Ravens' from his name," Pittsburgh Post-Gazette; January 14, 2009.

Nesbit, Joanne. "Roosevelt may be 'father of annual Army-Navy football game'," The University Record, www.ur.umich.edu/0001/Sep11_00/11.htm, September 11, 2000.

Walker, James. "NFL: 'Financial obligation remains' before Ocho Cinco on jersey," www.espn.com, September 7, 2008.

Index

INDEX

INDEX